Elder Skelter

Elder Skelter

Jan Seale

Copyright 2024 @ Jan Seale
All Rights Reserved

ISBN: 978-1-962148-10-8
LOC: 2024940787
Editor: Christine Osborne
Cover Design: Erren Seale

Lamar University Literary Press
Beaumont, TX

Older?
It's who you've always been, only later.

Recent Poetry from Lamar University Literary Press

Lisa Adams, *Xuai*
Walter Bargen, *Radiation Diary: Return to the Sea*
Christine Boldt, *In Every Tatter*
Devan Burton, *A Room for Us*
Jerry Bradley, *Collapsing into Possibility*
Mark Busby, *Through Our Times*
Julie Chappell, *Mad Habits of a Life*
Stan Crawford, *Resisting Gravity*
Glover Davis, *Academy of Dreams*
Wendy Dunmeyer, *My Grandmother's Last Letter*
Chris Ellery, *Elder Tree*
Kelly Ann Ellis, *The Hungry Ghost Diner*
Dede Fox, *On Wings of Silence*
Alan Gann, *That's Entertainment*
Larry Griffin, *Cedar Plums*
Lynn Hoggard, *First Light*
Michael Jennings, *Crossings: A Record of Travel*
Markham Johnson, *Dear Dreamland*
Betsy Joseph & Chip Dameron, *Relatively Speaking*
Jim McGarrah, *A Balancing Act*
J. Pittman McGehee, *Nod of Knowing*
David Meischen, *Caliche Road Poems*
Laurence Musgrove, *A Stranger's Heart*
Benjamin Myers, *The Family Book of Martyrs*
Janice Northerns, *Some Electric Hum*
Godspower Oboido, *Wandering Feet on Pebbled Shores*
Dave Oliphant, *Summing Up: Selected Poems*
Nathaniel O'Reilly, *Landmarks*
Carol Coffee Reposa, *Sailing West*
Steven Schroeder, *the moon, not the finger, pointing*
C.W. Smith, *The Museum of Marriage*
Vincent Spina, *The Sumptuous Hills of Gulfport*
W.K. Stratton, *Betrayal Creek*
Ken Waldman, *Sports Page*
Loretta Diane Walker, *Ode to My Mother's Voice*
Dan Williams, *At the Gates, a Refuge of Milkweed and Sunflowers*
Jonas Zdanys, *The Angled Road*

For information on these and other Lamar University Literary Press books go to www.Lamar.edu/literarypress

Acknowledgements

Thanks to the editors of the following publications for their acceptance and first publication of some of the poems in this book:

Bearing the Mask: Southwestern Persona Poems
Lone Star Poetry
The Parkinson Poems
Phoebe
Quotable Texas Women
Texas Poetry 8
Texas Poetry Assignment
Texas Poetry Ballots
Voices de la Luna
The Wonder Is
Writing Texas
The Yin of It

Contents

I. Connecting the Dots

13	Connections
14	Sailing Over the Moon in Texas
16	My Friend A.R. Writes
17	To a Friend Across Town
18	My Friend JoAnne Replies
19	The San Antonio Daily Light Interviews Madam Candelaria
21	The Elephant in the Room
23	Apology for a Non-letter
25	Sizing Up Us Girls
26	Soft Shoe and Whistling with my Mother-in-law
27	One Sunday Morning

II. Patronizing the Flesh

31	On Forgetting Names
33	Cataracts
34	Waterways
35	Trimmed Extremity
36	Fair Exchange
37	Non-compliant
38	Crone Texture
39	Annual Checkup
40	What I Learned on My Broken Hip Vacation
41	On the Hospital Room Ceiling
42	Hospital Lesson
43	Deceleration
44	Glimpse through a Rest Home Door
45	The Nobility of Canes
46	Mole
47	Chronometry
48	How Bible Verses Are Rescuing Me

III. Playing the Field

51	Gravity
52	In Lieu of Watching Wildlife in Africa
53	Letting It All Hang Out
54	Voting by Mail
55	Lifelong Learning
56	Playing the Flute After Long Absence

57	Viewing Rembrandt's Old Women
59	Argument: Mesquite Bean Coffee vs. Arabian Coffee
61	Winter Texans
63	Savoring
64	A Blessing for Writing Utensils
65	The Zen of Jigsaw Puzzles
66	Ten Commandments for Older Writers

IV. Circling the Wagons

69	We Help Each Other Be Old
70	Shade
71	Deciduous
72	A Woman's Body, Remembering
74	Moment After Childbearing Years
75	Handwriting on the Wall
76	Family Portrait
77	Self-talk
78	Old Woman's Song from Mesa Verde
79	Predictions
80	Pre-need
82	Suddenly...
83	Later
84	Prognostication
85	Seasoned Love

I.

Connecting the Dots

A faithful friend is the medicine of life.
—*Ecclesiastes 6:16*

Connections

Why oh why do I think of Margaret
when I wash my face? Why does George,
who died not long ago,
come to mind when I use the calculator?
Janis is a corn casserole.
Elizabeth helps walk the dog.
You get the picture.
I once thought I was moving toward
certifiable, a few more free associations
and I'd be taken but kindly away.
Now I'm fine, since I learned
from a lesson on the brain
how the ends of synapses may go visiting,
whip their tentacles about a memory
lurking in another part of the brain.
It's only a game, to see who wants
to belong to what.
Couplings. Duos. Partners.

Sailing Over the Moon in Texas
for Charles

How you called from Dallas to see if
I was still coming to the Texas State Fair,
how I said I'd lost the will, then you told me
about your tests for vertigo, and at the end
of possible diagnoses we wondered silently
if this was not the beginning of ailments
finally halting the merriment of friendship;

how I suddenly remembered the lunar eclipse
beginning at 9:11 (why, oh why that time?)
and, not wanting our connection broken,
how we hurried out to our respective lawns,
phones pressed to our heads, looking east,
you dodging fir and elm, I palm and mesquite,
and began to co-narrate the celestial event;

how it was a luminous fingernail at first,
yet I observed the other side faintly glowing.
(You could not see the other side prompting you
to say you had not had your glasses changed
in several years. Well, then no wonder, I said,
but it's just a fingernail, though I willed you
to see the umbra and after a while, you did);

how the fingernail was trimmed by the earth,
bursting in with the astronomy scissors,
while we asked, Is it smaller where you are?
Laughing, as if we could know...then Nah,
the distance between us is nothing at all
compared to the earth from the moon tonight,
hugging as it is, the short side of its ellipsis.

And though we didn't make Guinness,
I awoke next morning to think of the numbers:
60 years between us since high school,
500 miles the road between us,
220,000 miles the moon's wink,
we in a giant triangulation with it
from our respective driveways,
leaning, pointing, straining, blinking,

what with your vertigo, my bad ear,
your heart valve, my heartache,
thinking this might be our only time
to share a celestial event;
but how maybe next year we could try
to close in on the state fair,
say howdy to Big Tex, see the sheep exhibit,
eat deep-fried anything, and ride
the round moon of the Ferris wheel together.

My Friend A.R. Writes
a found poem

I have nightmares. Dreams fascinate.
I try to remember some, even write the details
in the middle of the night. With that crutch
I can reconstruct. They always have people
from my many lives in them. And they don't know
each other. I am always an observer, thinking
"You can't be having lunch—
you don't even know each other."

To a Friend Across Town

I think of you fairly often,
and guilt invades my day
like a tiny ant running over
a sleeve.

We had our weekly Fridays
at the uptown Starbucks.
The other days of the week
I thought of things to tell you,
some of which I know now
you didn't care to hear.

Why don't I call you?
Why don't I do better
with our friendship?
It has to do
with my new friend—
a body propped up,
watched carefully over.

It has to do with
an immediacy
of appointments.
My neglect of you is because
my days come up short,
because my time is spent
remembering small tasks.

I am saying your name carefully.
I am saying your husband's
and children's names
with effort.
I wait to be a better friend,
whatever that means,

except now my hair needs a comb,
coffee must be made,
the world news worried over.
So forgive my absence,
this day-after-fleeting-day
silence. For now, I can only
offer you this comfort:
Know you are
special in my neglect.

My Friend JoAnne Replies
a found poem

Yes, it would be wonderful
to have a long talk
about middle and old age
and what you kindly call
exchanging vitality for wisdom.
Me? I've been looking at it
as being too pooped to give
a rat's patootie and therefore
letting go of things—both
those I can't control, and
a lot of those that I can.

The San Antonio Daily Light Interviews Madam Candelaria in 1895

Sit right there at porch edge—right square
in front of me. My ears have outlived me.
I will need to see your mouth for questions.
So. I'll do my best but it was long ago.
No, my little *perro* will not bite.
Gordita she is, fat as the ones I served
the Texians and Tejanos when they came
to my hotel to eat, to dance the fandango,
mingle, enjoy themselves. Who knew,
come six days later, they would all be dead?
Claro! I saw it all. Listen to me well
for they tell me I am one hundred and ten—
no one else is left. *Mi cuento es doloroso*
and it will be double in my heart if I learn
you wrote the wrong words in the news.

I was Andrea Castañon Villanueva. Still,
married to a Candelario, who could resist
being renamed? But this reminds me,
General Houston wrote me a note, called me
"Candelarita," said, "go to Bowie in the Alamo."
We all knew the situation was *difícil, muy difícil*,
noise for days—smoke and clamor, shouting.
What was to become of San Antonio de Bexar?
The messenger slipped through in the night,
knocking, then calling softly, *"Ven rápido!"*
I took a sack, filled it with aloe spears,
with *manzanilla* leaves, a jug of water,
soft rags, a *piloncillo* to sweeten the pain.
In a side room he was, poor man on a cot,
his face bright hot, his eyes a-glitter.
"Ah, Madam Candelaria, you have come,"
he said, and laid his head against me.
I put water to the lips, a cool cloth to brow—
(Aieee! My own rheumy body pains me
as I think of his suffering—Here, Gordita,
sit on my feet—a little dog helps.)

I could hear gunshots, the Mexicanos' shouts
as they came near despite the pleas
of Travis to let a dying man alone. Pardon my tears—

they never cease to come when I tell this part:
Such though he was, Bowie insisted on firing
his firearm, over and over, only to fall back,
entreating my help to reload. One last time,
and his body went slack in my arms.
The typhoid had claimed him. At once,
the Mexicanos burst into the room, coming at us
with their bayonets. *"Por el amor de Dios,"*
I screamed, "don't spoil a dead man's body!"

As they bore down on him—Come close—
they grazed me here—See the scar on my face?
No? I assure you it is no wrinkle of age.
I've borne it 59 years. Wait, I'll wipe my tears—
I'll stand, lean over toward you…Right there…
Um hunh…you see? And while I'm standing,
you are welcome to drop a coin or two
into the pocket of this old apron I always wear.

Thank you, and send your friends around.
I can tell this saddest of stories many ways.

Madam Candelaria, an innkeeper in San Antonio at the time of the battle at the Alamo, is thought to have been brought into the Alamo when it was under siege in order to nurse James Bowie, ill with a fever. She lived to be 113 and told her story in lively drama to tourists and journalists.

The Elephant in the Room

I was driving him to the doctor when Dad
saw them first, two elephants in a plowed field.
Chained to stakes, they were calmly eating hay,

blurring the scene in Hannibal abruptness.
A circus hand sat on a stool nearby.
Dad was beside himself. "How come?"

he said over and over. "Are we seeing things?"
Later he told my mother about the elephants
and then a neighbor. For all he knew,

they were Ganeshas, pachyderm gods of India.
He could only shake his head in disbelief,
telling and re-telling the vision all day

to anyone who would listen, smile at an old man's
possible delusion and utter confoundment.
I thought of how, when I was a girl,

he was cleaning the kitchen stove when
a vital spring slipped from a valve, spewing gas,
which hitched a ride on the pilot light,

then sprang roaring orange to the ceiling.
Dad reached his hands into the flame,
reattached the spring, saved our house and us.

(Why do I remember Mother and me
in the doorway, astounded and screaming,
Mother holding toilet paper in one hand?)

For several weeks he wore the gauze mitts
of those badly burned, elephantine hands
swathed in white. We did everything for him.

Mother did the personal things, and I?
I got to feed him, gauging when he would
want another bite, and of which food.

But my favorite job was turning
the pages of the book he was reading,
"Now," he'd say, or "Okay, sweetie."

Twenty years later he fed me supper
as I gingerly propped myself upright,
having just given him his first grandson.

He was smiling, smiling at the occasion,
both novel and grand, perhaps stirring an
old memory of feeding my toddler-self.

Later that night I heard his plane overhead,
clearing the city, him returning to work upstate,
his legacy assured, never forgetting the fact.

We may observe threads of spirit all around:
a triangle of glory in large mammals feeding,
father and daughter feeding each other,

chiming strains of grace, strong as house fires,
improbable as two circus beasts feeding
in a fallow cotton field one bright morning.

Apology for a Non-letter

I am writing to tell you
I will not be writing you
until I can present a united front.
Today I am in the down phase of my moon.
Yesterday the sun was too hot,
the cicadas screaming.
Today the ills are jostling for attention,
as if the silly discomforts are
making a case for themselves.
I am waiting to write you
until these preoccupations subside.

Today the world is spinning upside down,
various cultures saying "What?"
when they tumble into each other.
I will write you a real letter
when I am not biting my lips over this fact.

I will go on and on about our hummingbirds.
I will say we had doughnuts for breakfast.
I will report giant sunflowers in bloom
and tell you a story of an aunt who
reports a roadrunner bringing a lizard to her
at the back door promptly at 7 each a.m.

The truth is, lately four friends have died,
it has not rained for a month,
and we sleep poorly or not at all.

I am postponing inspiration,
hunting for good karma, kindness,
a way to bring you glad tidings of great joy.
I am waiting to write you without statistics,
without bellowing or ranting.
I am hanging back, going about my day,
a conversation with you in my head,
a memory of our three-hour breakfasts,
a shared poem, dogs we named and liked.

Someday the sun will be shining
without malevolence.
Birds will be gathering

at puddles of fresh rain.
I will open my heart to you,
where will be meaningful words
written on quality writing paper,
no dashed-off email
or a clipped text message.

Meanwhile, bear with me until
I can write the following—
as we were trained in 6th grade
to do for the salutatory greeting—
"Hello, how are you? I am fine."

Sizing Up Us Girls

My sister tells me on our weekly Sunday phone visit
that she has discovered she doesn't match side to side
after a fall that happened years ago.
I counter that one of my arms is longer than the other,
thank you, my own version of hit-and-try-to-run.
What would our mother think of us,
pins in her mouth, tape measure draping her,
threatening to slap us if we don't stand up straight,
wondering why the garment she is pinning on us
is all whomperjawed?

Soft Shoe and Whistling with my Mother-in-law

Today I put away your garters, scarves, sachet
you never thought yourself good enough to use.
Folding up your dresses, airy and full of flowers,
took a long time, a certain quaintness in it all.
You left a tissue in each pocket, often a grocery list,
phone number. There were dresses you intended to wear,
some you overwore, favorites ready like anxious puppies.
I keep myself reasonable, at high tide all day
not to spoil the job.

Into eight boxes I have put the round and malleable you,
as Picasso might send his tender blue woman on the shore
up the harsh stairs of Avignon, or as the difference
in your breasts when you would lie down,
the real one heading for comfort beside your silky inner arm,
the other, fashioned of plastic,
stubborn as a mountain over the mass of scars.
I took your prosthesis with your burial clothes,
then was sorry to see it stiff and ridiculous on your chest
like a separate casket for your given-out heart.

For three weeks I have carried you in a bundle in my head.
Tonight your wavy gray hair, green eyes are an aquarium
among the periwinkles, roses, fleurs-de-lis of your dresses.
I lie down in the boxes that will be taken tomorrow,
smell the faint odor meaning you,
love you out of my generation, as my sister.
I ask for some strength you let go of,
your 70 years to take me places I have not been.
You call to me over the powder dish, the brooches,
saying a woman's life is worth living for,
saying never mind the stiff breast we could not fix,
saying it lies pinned to you now like a medal of honor.

One Sunday Morning

I.

When my son and I head west upriver early on a Sunday in spring we come upon a story: fifty humans walking the east-bound lane in silence, families in front—mothers holding swaddled babies, fathers with toddlers beside—youths to the rear with backpacks, their shoes aflop with no laces. Slow trucks of the Border Patrol, one leading, another following, shepherd the line. These humans have crossed nation to nation in the night and come up from the Rio at daybreak, cheered on by mesquite, huisache, ebony.

II.

An hour passes and we arrive at our own destination on the Rio Grande. We finish our official business but hesitate to leave, walking a block in this post-colonial town until we eye a caliche path that descends the embankment. It seems to be a service road angled from street level down to the Rio Grande's edge. "Mother, do you think you can do this?" my son solicits. I'm willing to try. Holding on to each other, we inch our way down, feeling ourselves being studied on a distant screen. Still, no uniforms or flashing lights, no gates, walls, or demands of credentials. We find ourselves under the bridge, an oasis between nations, a few permitted cars clunking overhead—perhaps to deliver bread, the Mass, or visiting *abuelas*. Across the water, in the determined Mexican town, church bells start up, activate baying dogs. The morning breeze from the Gulf reaches miles upriver to skim cool over the water. Two Mexican children swish-dance around the bridge pillars. Dare we a moment of grace? There's more.

III.

We turn our gaze upward, where a thousand mud bowls surprise us, a tightly woven mural on the bridge underbelly. Swallows have sought out this manmade contraption, glued their ceramic nests, obscuring the girders, the concrete, the stays. Now birds dart, soar, happy with the morning's feed, returning to their chicks through the mouths of their grinning mud gourds, each choosing its own.

IV.

   This, this, we say, is what it means to take hold of peace: sunrise yellowing the day, water speaking prudence, air breathing kindness, the duet of swallow wings and children's laughter. All here between nations. We think of the humans we saw earlier on the highway who have crossed this morning filled with fear and hope, and of those who receive them in dutiful patience day in, day out. How the birds give, in their innocent tight formation of nests, the definition of neighbors. How the earth tells us that the way things fit is what we must know. How this moment comes saying connection, connection.

II.

Patronizing the Flesh

It is in truth a most contagious game:
Hiding the Skeleton shall be its name.
—*George Meredith*

On Forgetting Names

I am unable to name my favorite professor
just now, though I vowed at the time
I would never forget him. It is Dr. _____.
The alphabet is roamed: "B" or "D" or later "S"?
I am leaning into a "W." I make a coffee,
spread it across an early morning hour,
give his name over to my other self,
the one always in control, ever bent on
playing tricks on the me writing this.

He smoked constantly, one foot
propped on the professorial chair,
leaning on the spare knee with one arm.
He listened, smoked, listened
to our early poetic ravings,

later wisely told us how to improve
this or that idea, wondered if this particular
stanza would go better in another place?
(likely the trash, but he'd never say it)
He didn't stop Tom from critiquing,
saying it like it was, usually
"This poem is shit, throw it away."
Still, I'd come out later only bruised,
because Dr. _____ said it was just the one line
that was "troubling."
I heard later that he died,
as all favorite people seem to,
that it was from smoking too much
(no doubt while listening to our Creative Writing).
Still, I wonder if he was happy

or a frustrated poet, agreeing principally
with his maker to listen to others' poems,
precious and adolescent as they were,
and did he forget, at the last, all our names.
and what did they do with his fan mail,
from me and one other in the group?

And did that other also forget his name
but adored him through the years?
Now for the therapeutic nature of writing poems,

he would say it was because I had struggled,
struggled through the delectable
memory built into a poem that I am now
rewarded to find him waiting for me here at the end,
beside memory's classroom door:
Dr. Webster.

Cataracts

Our eyes gleam in the mirror like a cat's
who's furtively crossing a street at night.
Little squares of light dancing unbidden,
they startle younger friends with
a mere nod of the head, a blink,
a lamp lit across a room.
These bits out us when we least expect.

Earlier, the oculist says he's never heard
it put like this: seeing pink in one eye,
blue in the other. Nevertheless,
thus begins the new hardware.

At night we lie down,
close our patched eyes,
think of the glass therein,
glad for the help,
remembering a great-grandfather
sitting on the porch in his undershirt,
his hat on, expecting to go
to some magical place
where he could at last see.

Waterways

Time creates a new geography of the body,
rivulets, canals, depressions absent before,
the laughter of gravity, creases speaking right up
that they need drying, that they will cry
if put away wet, hidden in stretchy clothes.
No raging rivers, they're simple channels,
banks of tired skin with no place to go,
rills and runnels saying hello to old flesh,
neighborhoods forgotten after the bath,
whiners for the towel.

Trimmed Extremity

"Here's a bad poem," I say to my son
as we wait in the emergency room.
"A broken humerus is not humorous."
He says, "I've already thought of that."
Later now, my pen chatters, hiccups,
pleading for a pain reliever.
Too late, I'm reminded I've been guilty
of taking the body's interior for granted.

This morning in the orthopedist's office,
we sat, a whole room of us,
our worlds slowed toward zero,
gloomy, resigned, bored, in pain:
a man with an iron foot,
a woman atop a gigantic pillow,
an arm-casted kid with a worried father,
and I with my limp purple arm,
all awaiting salvation for our limbs.

Soon there's an announcement:
"Sorry, folks, the doctor has left
for a serious case."

We heave ourselves toward the door,
our club meeting broken up.
On the way to the car, I try to drum up cheer.
After all, what's a broken arm doing
acting important in a broken world?
A broken arm can still breathe, does not
have to go to war, its climate change
of purple eventually recovering.
A broken arm is only me and it,
is only personal, its hurt merely mine.
My arm says it's right to feel like granite.
Au contraire, the world is broken, bored,
needs re-casting, may develop complications,
may not make it.

Soup tonight, sent by miracle across country
by people knowing supper is essential:
delicious chicken poblano soup, creamy,
swirling with bits of peppers, forgiving evil,
flattering the tongue. Arm medicine.

Fair Exchange

The mobile x-ray man came this morning
to x-ray my broken arm. He was quick. It was painless.
He gave me his card, saying if I ever needed
a digital x-ray,
an ultra-sound,
a 2D-echo,
a vascular,
or an EKG,
just call him.

I thought of giving him my card,
if he ever needed
a sonnet,
a quatrain,
some couplets,
a villanelle,
a limerick,
or a ballad,
that is,
as soon as I could write again.

Non-compliant

My left arm refuses to reach out when I tell it to,
gone into a permanent pout on being smashed
on a walkway booby-trapped with a concrete block.
A year later, it has settled into stubborn willfulness.
Oh, it will agree to write these words, swing
when the owner is walking, allow sleep as long as
it's not pressed into the pillow. What it will not do:
reach into a cupboard, comb hair in the back,
vote "by a show of hands," carry a heavy sack,
give another a full body embrace and a back pat,
conduct business through the window at the ATM,
agree to be a twin to the other arm.

Crone Texture

I tastefully protest.

"But I *am*," she says again.

And she makes me agree.

Then we spend a gentle while
naming other things wrinkled:

>   sand dunes
>   a newborn's scalp
>   ripples on a pond
>   a bloodhound's brow
>   the chambered nautilus
>   clouds
>   folds of silk

Annual Checkup

I am preparing for a doctor visit,
documenting my list of ills.
Before I go, I practice speaking
this inventory in eight minutes.
He will not look at me
while I am talking.
He will be hard at work
on his computer.
I won't know if he's
consulting Medicare.
Regardless, he is rapt.
When I'm through
disgorging my complaints,
he will rise, promise tests
and prescriptions, exit
without what I think of
as an old-fashioned goodbye.

What I Learned on My Broken Hip Vacation

Getting in and out of bed is a complex operation.
Some walkers are too wide for bathroom doors.
A great pedicure is possible with a broken hip.
Affection-giving will be optional and creative.
People tend to stare at walker-walkers.
Buttocks may not match each other.
Hip-breakers will learn dependency.
Hips are boring but vital hinges.

On the Hospital Room Ceiling

One large yellow triangular sign says
        CALL
     DON'T FALL
Another in Spanish admonishes
       LLAME
      NO SE
       CAIGA
They are no-nonsense messages.
They are there for me to think about.
I have plenty of time for such.
Since they are side by side,
could a patient read the two of them
simultaneously, one for each eye?
True bilingual. True Tex-Mex.
And what kind of help if one called—
With the Spirit? With a plunge of hope?
I stop thinking, look out the window
where a comical grackle has landed,
is looking at himself in the glass.
I am safe again.

Hospital Lesson

I asked Daniel,
who was tending
the beeping machine
beside my bed,
"What's a PCT?"
After all, his name
was paired with it
on a wall board
across from my feet.
There was a pause,
while he worked to
silence the irritant.
Then a reply,
"It's like a CNA."

Deceleration

My father did a great imitation of Tim Conway in his little old man character on the Carol Burnett Show. It took years, but the silliness and smiles accompanying that parody melded into a true-to-life scene, with Dad shuffling about the house in tiny steps. What once made us laugh became the sobering imperative.

How slowly we walk, not because we can't walk faster, but so we will not lose our balance and fall.

Yesterday we went for a walk in a park with a visiting son and became aware of the difference in our gaits. He would sprint ahead, then turn, pause, wait for us to catch up, sometimes checking in with a caller on his phone.

Glimpse through a Rest Home Door

What pleasure's left to love
but being smoothed with cream?
Her daughter's hands run
up and down her arms,
replacing a man's
on her thighs.

So it is,
pudding on the tongue,
a flashy potted violet,
a child's cry in the hall
that years ago
she would answer quick.

Now, all thought,
reason, philosophy, faith
sit with her only as a touch,
a sigh, an old picture mounted
on the wall *sans* frame.

The Nobility of Canes

When you first use the Medicare cane—
the J-cane, the ortho-, or the quad,
do not let it be your bane.
Pretend you're walking like a god.

Moses, turning his staff to snake,
King Lear, fleeing sad old age,
Paul Bunyan with his walking stick,
Charles Dickens in a streetside rage;

Lady Astor with a dog's head handle,
Tenzing Norgay with a trekking pole,
Socrates in the Senate in sandals,
Falstaff tapping the stage in his role;

Shepherd with crook on Christmas night,
Mary Poppins' umbrella handy,
Warrior with rapier flashing bright,
Gangster with prop for sipping brandy.

Do not walk gimpy or out of joint.
Prestige, status, momentum gain.
Clinch it, tap it, whack it, point
when you accept your Medicare cane.

Mole

Not the kind tunneling under a lawn,
making some New Englander mad,
or a spy in the government,
but a spot on the back
tunneling out from the interior,
poking its head up just below
the left shoulder. It was there
a while before the wearer saw it,
avoiding the backward look
with a mirror as one is prone to do.
So, hello, punctuation mark,
commentary on the backside
telling one she is only half awake
about her insides, unaware
of the forces jumping outside immunity.
The dermatologist pronounces you harmless,
"Something we get as we age," she says
from out of her perfect complexion.
We suppose we should thank you for
not choosing the middle of the face.
Here's the question: Do you have friends
eager to go onstage?

Chronometry

The hardest thing to comprehend is the passage of time. That passing is lauded when we're admiring how a child grows, how teens make it through the rocky years, how beautiful is the photo of young families, how people become skilled in their jobs.

Then "old" comes on the scene. Now everything is harder, more complex, not "like it used to be." So with organs having passed their prime, eyesight dimming, bones rubbing against each other. We use energy—energy that was joyfully spent earlier—to try to put the skids on time. Vitamins, exercise, diaries, memory tricks. In a thousand ways we say, "Time, listen to me. No! I said No!"

How Bible Verses Are Rescuing Me

"Seek and ye shall find"
I say, searching for a lost earring.

"Be ye kind, one to another"
I tell a driver who honks at me.

"Jesus wept"
I remind myself when one eye waters.

"The last shall be first"
when I clear a door held open for me.

These handles float up while
I give belated thanks
to a stern-lipped teacher
who planted them in my brain,
knew I'd need them some day.

III.

Playing the Field

Play up! Play up! and play the game!
—*Sir Henry John Newbolt*

Gravity

Yes, it helps us stick to the earth,
blotting paper or glue that never dries.
Yet its absence is exhilarating,
like Sally Ride's hair full of body,
or the faces of returning astronauts
echoing eternity as aliens
in the capsule's doorway.

For those of us remaining on earth,
what we might modestly prefer
is an important piece of paper
afloat at eye level,
crumbs around the table
reverting to the whole loaf,
an antique vase undropped,
a child with no skinned knees,
an elder unscathed by a misstep.

Instead, we remain gumshoes,
sympathizers with Icarus.
We must weigh situations,
drag toward solutions, understand
that the film cannot be reversed.
What's to do short
of breaking the bonds of earth?

Let us observe the trees, ancients
whose roots capitalize downward,
how small animals are not afraid
of the magnetism of their lairs.
Let us credit Newton for the marriage
of celestial bodies and apples falling.

Feeling the knock of moonlight at a window,
or the suck of high tide sifting our toes,
everything tended, all matter soothed
with strange logic, let us bless
the pull that bids us lie down each night,
gravitate toward being embraced,
first by the earth, then by each other.

In Lieu of Watching Wildlife in Africa

A tinny clank-clank disturbs my dream.
I rise for a mad, officious look.
Outside our bedroom, a possum
is eating the bird's suet block.
The suet cage swings against
the window guard. I find this
adolescent possum incurably cute.
Returning to bed, I face a dilemma:
Who gets my conservation vote
at sunrise? This ball of fur,
with velvet ears working madly,
or the thirteen noisy sparrows
fighting off one another's lust?

Letting It All Hang Out

The big question is the IT,
supposing IT has to be ALL.
And there must be permission,
telling IT goodbye,
checking ITs dangling apparatus.

And the next big question:
If IT is hanging, doesn't IT
have to be hanging by something?
What about the part still inside?
Who will grant that permission?
Who will hold on tight to ITs tail?
This slogan begins to doubt itself.

Will the remaining part left behind,
the one that allows the hanging,
be eternally jealous? After ALL,
IT gets that wonderful flapping
in the wind, and light, and
best of ALL, lack of closure.

The operative impossible is "HANG."
There must always be a hand
to dangle IT, or a book weighting IT
on the ledge. Always, a show time.
The truth is, there will always be
another ALL to hang out.

Voting by Mail

I dedicate...
...my pristine clean and easy vote
coming to mailbox in green election envelope,
returned in white ballot envelope,
inside yellow carrier envelope
to those on election day:
a mother whose baby seems to gain weight
in her arms while she stands in the queue;
a man who has worked a day flagging cars
now swaying to soothe his tired feet;
a young woman blinking at sun in her eyes
while the wind entangles her hair;
a lettuce handler, first time voting,
who worries he'll be late clocking in.
I dedicate my vote to an old woman shifting
a purse heavy with unneeded credentials;
to an old man bound in a van wheelchair
who awaits poll watcher, poll worker, assistant
advancing kindly with portable voting machine.

Lifelong Learning

I remember a visit with my parents when they were in their eighties. I suggested some activity where we could enjoy new information—a film, a museum, a lecture, an educational outing of some sort—and my mother replied, "But I don't want to learn anything new." I probably just huffed and marched out of the room. I know I went home shocked, dismayed, flummoxed at my mother's indifference.

Now, only now, do I think I understand her attitude. She went straight to the question: Why? What is the purpose of learning when one is old? Will it be "useful" in the sense of being able to apply it in a practical sense, something besides entertaining others at a party? I can think of a few retorts to my evil twin posing the questions.

The biggest reason for investigating, spending time with new stuff? It's fun. Entertaining. Passing the time (of which we don't have a great store of) in a way that gives instant reward. Learning the names of the red-eyed vireo or Thai basil makes me feel smarter, gives me something to chew on, makes me wonder who applied that particular moniker.

In this world of daily changing technology, we know if we want to communicate with our grandchildren, we'd better have a little up-to-date knowledge in our pocket, or at least know enough to ask them to define a term or help us with a move on our telephone or computer.

I make a point to ask my carry-out grocery kid something about his or her life. "Are you in school?" "What's your major?" "Will you stay in this area?" Besides doing my Girl Scout good deed of the day by showing interest in a struggling youth, I want to know, to find out what a major in "game design" might be, how a junior in college is already doing his student teaching, what degree of training it takes to become an EMS, why oh why does one still want to become a Border Patrol officer.

The best reason for old-age curiosity is a completely selfish one. Learning is brain food. Researchers tell us we need to move those brain parts around, stretch, replace, enhance them in order to stay alive. Learning may make the legs work better, certainly the tongue and the eyes and ears.

Long live the crossword puzzle! The lecture on aqua science! The thousand-piece jigsaw puzzle! Thumbing through the old dictionary or zipping to Google!

Go find out something new. Then excogitate and perpend on it. (Dictionary please.)

Playing the Flute After Long Absence

The silver is the first to hear the tone
and then the lip decides it too can like
the mellowness that slices like a knife
the silent air on which the note is blown.
The player feels the burden all alone
to shine the tarnished piping back to life.
Strangely, as the notes pile to the light,
the tune, like water, seeks its own.
The fingers gain a temporary cure
from arthritis, dull procrastination;
the embouchure minds its reputation.
Sculptured sound recalls it can be pure.
It cancels out the sin of hesitation,
restores the flutist's sonorous sensation.

Viewing Rembrandt's Old Women

I. Head of an Aged Woman

She has rheumy eyes, downcast.
He covers her with an apron, a sash,
a coat, a hood, and a mantle. Creases
around her lips, a bulbous nose,
withered cheeks show he is looking closely.
She doesn't mind holding still.

II. Portrait of a Seated Old Woman with Clasped Hands

They are not truly clasped:
one is splayed flat on the table,
the other holds the wrist of the splayed.
She is pale, with lines in her forehead.
She has agreed to sit for two penningen.
He loves her only for her artistic promise.
She is using the time for contemplation.

III. Old Woman Praying

She is frozen in devotion,
but he honors her with a red hood,
bits of red on wrists, bosom,
shoulder. Of course, her eyes are closed.
Why she has her mouth open
showing she has only lower teeth
is Rembrandt's private knowledge.
Maybe she can't bite God this way.

IV. Portrait of Rembrandt's Mother

It's an etching, all right,
with way too much liberty
for lines, wrinkles, bulging eyelids,
crepey eyebrows, lips that have
already disappeared.
Did she get to see it: Say
"Rem, I don't think so"?
She knew better, that later,
she'd live immortal and the world
proclaim her "incredibly beautiful."

V. Old Beggar Woman with a Gourd
    a found poem

"Hand-pulled antique etching
framed by the artist himself.
Hooray! This order ships free."

Argument: Mesquite Bean Coffee vs. Arabian Coffee

Why would you do this, take a holy
popular elixir and borrow its name?

> Who said coffee must be made
> with a strict heritage from Africa?

Why not call mesquite bean coffee
Mesquite-aide or Bean Consommé?

> Why call your coffee Transfusion?
> Jitter Juice? Java? Joe?

But couldn't this go trending, spreading
to pinto or lima or green pea coffee...

> Is there a license, a copyright
> for black, comforting, exotic?

...maybe sneaking on to carrot coffee,
radish coffee, tomato coffee?

> Oh come now, aren't we getting
> a bit defensive and upset?

But what does it look like, this sipped
stuff before it is brewed?

> If you must know, like fine sand,
> with a few twigs, mere shreds.

Has anyone asked permission to grind beans
and pods, offer the resulting concoction?

> Could you stop making distinctions,
> just be open-minded and tolerant?

Liquid trash trees! Cow feed! That's what it is!
Vaqueros out on the range with *nada* else.

> Look: It isn't against the law,
> heretical, unhealthy, or misnamed.

No stimulant? Depression could set in,
upending the universe, stopping civilization.

>   Here. Calm yourself. Take a sip.
>   Consider it a peace offering.

Winter Texans

Snowbirds they have always been called
but lately a new moniker: Q-tips,
that is, snow-white hair on head,
white tennies on feet. Call them either,
face to face, they will laugh agreement.
Nothing bothers these folks in annual migration.

Taking the great southern route each autumn,
like birds migrating to warmer climes,
they command Winnebagos and Airstreams,
or, waiting for them in countless parks,
air out their 'park model' homes.
They're planning reunions, square dancing,
card games, shuffleboard, ping pong.

Calloused hands from fifty years of farming,
making biscuits, feeding chickens, or
curved backs from sitting at a desk all day,
eyes dimmed with necessary reading of
reports and student papers, they've come
to escape five months of shoveling snow.
But old habits die hard and they'll end up
tutoring children in the Valley's schools,
renovating houses for the poor,
crocheting caps for windy blasts,
sewing quilts for the over-traveled.
Some will ladle out kettles of hot soup
for the hopers and wishers.

They've put in storage or given away
their life clutter, are learning Spanish,
picking oranges, holding Saturday sales,
wading in the Gulf surf, driving to Mexico
for medicine, curios, haircuts, *cervezas*.

They'll do crosswords, bridge, movies until
Wednesday night, when they'll gather
in the clubhouse for jams, with guitars, fiddles,
banjos, accordions. But first they'll eat King Ranch
casserole, Spanish rice, tacos, enchiladas,
top these off with rhubarb pie and pound cake.

In their spare time, they're writing their life stories,
reading crime novels, Westerns, recipe books,
knitting grandbaby sweaters, woodcarving,
painting scenes of palm trees, resacas.
They're filling the parks with bike rides,
the flea markets with curiosity and joke-making.
They're claiming pleasure while they can.

Snowbirds of a feather flock to Texas together,
while Q-tips, their spines toward Texas incline.

Savoring

This recipe for oatmeal cookies
required an army of ingredients:
two sugars, three flours, four spices,
plus time-out in the fridge.
I was just trying to be successful
at *something* that day.
Later, I watched a man, thin
and shaking with incurable disease,
reach for cookie after cookie.
He ate them in a greedy, boyish way.
His wife said, "Thank goodness
you brought them because I
don't like them and thus don't
make them." And I felt the day
go all shining and right.

A Blessing for Writing Utensils

Writing utensils fill my house, every room with a cup holding pens and pencils, sometimes two containers. These felt-tipped, cartridged, sharp-or-dull, chewed, capped, fat- or none-butted, weeping or stoically dry sticks hold stories of their origins. They come from trips, giftings, hotels, a few from office supply stores.

They come home with me for a future of uncertain adolescence, click-clicked to oblivion by the thumb of a deep thinker or, in the case of pencils, their heads sucked for their sweet leady essence even though your mother told you it would kill you to do that. You believed her until you learned that the Renaissance painters stayed alive long enough, through their lead poisoning, to make themselves a name in history.

With these instruments, you know there are lists to be made, poems to be written, doodles completed during dull phone conversations. These stylographs will experience twiddlings, scratchings, punchings, naps enforced in the bottom of purses, coat pockets, and desk drawers. There may be pet gnawings, baby wavings, music conducting, amateur tattoos, as well as a whole set of malfeasances. These activities, in addition to the goodness these scribers allow me: to remember my groceries and appointments, not to mention how they pick up on my mind in my journals or scrawl a flash line on the back of an envelope for a future poem.

May pens and pencils never become obsolete, though they have their electronic detractors and enemies, their thoughtless owners forsaking them for making words with type keys or voice recognition.

I love you, pens and pencils. Click on. Scratch on. Ride that paper! Yee-haw!

The Zen of Jigsaw Puzzles

Come in. Stop for a minute. Look at this puzzle
lying like an odalisque on the dining table.
See how the reds trot off to the corner
to be a sunset, others sprawled in the middle
as bougainvillea. Pieces lock hands, touch toes,
butt heads. There are pieces diffident to company,
standing off to one side, resisting connections.
Occasionally a snake will manifest. One night
we missed a piece, half-joked we should
call the company, demand a new one, then found
it later snuggled in the carpet. Another time,
the sprawling mess tricked us into laboring hours
past our bedtime. We would have gone earlier
but couldn't face defeat by the wily pieces.

Who are the people making these puzzles?
Are they off in a corner devising seven shades of blue,
interminable fur, green expanses of forests?
Do they stay up nights like we do, only on
the other side of creativity, as slave masters
laughing with hideous teeth at our bewilderment?
Maybe there's no human tease behind the frame
but giant machines groaning out magazine scenes,
Van Gogh, Central Park, stamp collections.

And what about the finished puzzle sprawled
on an essential surface, unable to yield space
to eaters or students or paper sorters?
The thing is holding itself together, interlocking,
clinching its teeth, enjoying a permanence
it never had in its box. It's saying crazy games
have a place in this world, spawned by madcap,
ennui, when finished may enjoy a small eternity.

Ten Commandments for Older Writers

I. Pick your strongest motive for writing and go for it.
(You don't have enough time left to get acquainted with alternatives.)

II. Love yourself enough to exercise your talent.
(Disregard the world of new distractions.)

III. Do not fill up your writing with profanities.
(We all know what they are; you are not a stand-up comic.)

IV. Give yourself and your assistant an occasional rest.
(You'll think better after time-out.)

V. Remember you are part of a family.
(Honor the memory of your parents and pay attention to your children.)

VI. Don't murder another writer's reputation with a nasty review.
(If you do, remember the Golden Rule can be applied both ways.)

VII. Refrain from committing adulteration.
(Don't pollute; keep your office clean so your mind will be clear.)

VIII. Do not steal the words, plots, characters of another author.
(It won't work: AI and other readers will catch your theft.)

IX. Avoid details about your neighbors' or friends' lives that they might recognize.
(Got it?)

X. Don't begrudge your writer friends' honors, awards, or New York Times listings.
(Congratulate them and mean it; then get on with your own writing.)

IV.

Circling the Wagons

But he who kisses the Joy as it flies
Lives in Eternity's sunrise.
—*William Blake*

We Help Each Other Be Old

They say the names are the first to go,
but which—first or last? Miriam or Johnson?
Noe or Gonzalez? It is important for some reason
I might find out later, when it's too late.
If it's Susan, it might mean Alzheimer's
but if it's Malofski, well, such can be forgiven.
Even the famous heart surgeon
can let it slide, discount it to stress.
(So where are my great feats of lifesaving?)
Right now, today—a bonus we all agree—
I should make a list of the dangers of
vitamin supplementation, whether not
enough B_2 otherwise known as riboflavin
is making me forget to phone my friend
but whether too much will cause
a tingling sensation in my lips.
Today I should walk three miles,
do crossword puzzles, conjugate French verbs.
"What do you do if your fingers start crooked?"
asks the lady beside me on the bus. Then,
"I sure love old age—especially the money."

Shade

How shade is a living being
making, reshaping itself all day,
calling folks to come stand in it,
cattle and horses seeking it out
in draws, under trees, on hillsides,
how dogs may move, move
subtly and without complaint
wherever shade chooses itself to be,
how the landscape primps,
fizzles, comments endlessly on
its nature all the day long,
how the dear dark takes over,
how the patterns rearrange,
how the quiet of the *nublado* may
strangle the happiness of pure sun,
how shadow brings along its sister,
coolness, prints us out as twins;
how we take no mind that
these changing shapes lying beside,
ahead, or behind us are visible time
passing, pools of respite,
forecasts of our ephemeral stay
on this spotted earth.

How the imprint of cloud
or plane or sudden bird
chasing across the land
fascinates us—
how it loads up dimension,
quietly supplies depth,
everything in the way of light
pronouncing itself on a surface,
how it tries, but can never
stand equal to gravity, oxygen—
slightly mocking, softly calling,
wary of being caught,
patient for its turn at surfaces.

Without it we would be paper dolls.

Deciduous

Autumn leaves will follow me all the days of my life.

Growing up in a little town in north Texas, I dived into piles of oak and maple leaves my father raked together. It was a rare permissible display of abandon, thrashing in those crisp pyramids.

Much later, when I was a mother, the leaves followed me into sorrow. Our son left his hamster's cage door open and the tabby helped herself. Lying on the floor disconsolate, the eight-year-old raised his head long enough to say, "I wish I was a dead leaf. That way I would fall off the tree. But also someone would step on me and crush me."

A few Octobers ago I went to Maryland for a workshop at a retreat center outside Silver Springs. The locals were defying the fear that had gripped the region in the siege of who was termed "the D.C. shooter." Fall leaves formed a river of yellow and red beneath us. Wouldn't it be fun to take some home to south Texas, to our semi-tropical eternal summer?

My companions were eager to help me find the best. Halfway through our outing there at the head of the Appalachian Trail, shots rang through the woods. We scurried for cover; it was probably a hunter. And my salvaged leaves made it home in a plastic bag, ready to be preserved between sheets of wax paper until I could share with my grandchildren their shouting colors and traceable shapes.

Here on the Tex-Mex border, we do not have any "leaf-peeper" tours such as New England features each fall. October brings our signal seasonal display. Jillions of tiny yellow stars appear on our streets and lawns, heralding the maturation of the Golden Rain Tree, an exotic that made its way into this tip of Texas and couldn't get enough of our hospitality.

By mid-October the plenteous trees are laden with small yellow boxes. Inside are the seeds for the lacey saplings that will dot our flower beds in spring. But first, the clusters slowly turn to a rich coral orange, then to dusty rose, lingering a while as the mascot of our official autumn.

So, here in the Lower Rio Grande Valley, with winter approaching, our "leaf show" begins in stars, then proceeds to paper-petalled origami boxes dallying in orange sunsets. Come November, on a gust of wind, they'll tumble down and scuttle off to find some fertile dirt, bearing hopes of descendants.

Not a bad way to know the autumn of life.

A Woman's Body, Remembering

A hot coin spoke from one side,
a dog of a backache sniped.
The legs were pillars of Samson,
and the head, a swarm of gnats.
Why then, do I miss you,
Aunt Flo, Little Visitor,
Ragtime Sally, Queen's X,
you who have taken yourself away,
tightlipped, silent?

Sometimes I lie in bed calling to you
from the second half of my life.
Remember me?
Remember my useful body?
You came to me, made me
a worker of the world each month,
told me—you comforting clock,
scenic calendar page,
baby maker/trouble maker,
cascade of moon juice,
Rorschach quilt—
that I was all right.

If I could,
I would curl into you for five days,
go sit in my little hut,
without men, without kitchen duty,
curl nights into you,
be an embryo of the moon;

I would begin with ocher clay,
move on to the true flush of poppies,
and finally, would-be baby pink,
all these colors in health—
on a canvas of winning landscape;
this would be folded in linen,
handled only with clean hands,
laid in a cedar trunk,
brought out on feast days
to show my daughters-in-law:
"This is the original stuff of your husband.
Now go and paint your own."

Today, my body remote as an elevated railway,
like soap, like the horizon,
my body wishes to remember.

God's bound to be a woman sometimes,
to think up this bright paint between the legs.
Where else is flowing blood the picture of health,
a lovely joke about the future?

Moment After Childbearing Years

In the OB-Gyn waiting room,
I sit down in the warm seat
of a young husband just vacating it
when his pregnant wife's name is called.
His man scent of Mexico cologne lingers.
I am a little surprised how delicious
is the warmth from his backside.
How alive this couple is,
she of the beautiful dark mane,
he of the tight jeans with keys attached.
But why is he going all the way with her?
Is it to comfort his wife, or to make sure
the doctor does not enjoy the occasion?
Maybe there is important family news.
Meanwhile, his warmth lingers.
I think I should reach for a magazine.
Instead, I sit, I think, I smile at my little self
stealing passage in this man-womb.

Handwriting on the Wall

Some days the words try to escape,
try to get themselves over too soon,
gulp down syllables taking too long to write.
"Concentration" wills itself to be "concention."
There is an "l" demanding to be crossed
while a "t" sits begging. The humps
of "n's" and "m's" insist on harrumphing
as "enmity" refuses to behave.
Tangling with the line below are "p's" and "j's."
Meanwhile, words that have always
been faithful with the guts of their vowels
now try to trick "a's" into "o's,"
"i's" into "e's." All this while our grandchildren
go to their parents for help deciphering
their birthday greetings in cursive,
as we stubbornly refuse to print the words
for their understanding and benefit.

Family Portrait

Certainly the white-haired grandparents
with their naturally rounded bellies
will have dropped out of the picture

but what of the father on the left
who sired the four almost-tall teenagers?
He is absent by way of a troubled heart

and his daughter in short shorts
as befitting the summer day this picture
was taken now gone to some heaven

the rest of us have not. Another father
far right, contributing the three sprouting lads?
A ghost, only his music remaining.

Two sisters, who started it all, smile giddy,
hold hands in the success of the outing.
The six who are left have long been stretched out

of their teenage skins, stretched to a day's work
and incurable conditions, to poor plumbing
and trips to the vet and the hardware store,

to the band hall and the football game. But
look at them here in their matching striped shirts,
one boy on his knees (so as to get everyone

in the picture) who doesn't know that he's kneeling
in prayer for the falling away of the principals
and for his car-wrecked big sister, for the

eventual falling away of everyone here to make room
on the photographic paper for the next batch
to come cheerfully, innocently, to occupy

the frame, which is in fine condition even
after so many years and can be refilled again
and again on this pale blue dot sailing the sky.

Self-talk

I've gone to look up the phone number at my desk. Now I'm repeating it aloud as I go through the house looking for my phone. Does the recipe call for 1/2 teaspoon cinnamon, or is it ginger? I say the correct ingredient as I cross the kitchen. Page 272, that's where I need to head in the book after I've looked in the index.

Why do we talk to ourselves like this? Did I always say numbers, names, dates aloud? I think not. What I am thinking is that my brain is a big piece of dough sitting on the top of my neck. And it needs a knead of memory to operate properly in my present, long-time world.

Older folks have valid reasons to speak aloud to themselves. Maybe they're alone and need a companionable voice. Maybe they have harder problems to solve. Maybe they can't see the directions, the words as easily and need to program them into the auditory as quickly as possible. Maybe they've found out they are their own best friend and constant companion.

My mother, who lived longer than I am presently alive, was a master self-whisperer. She told herself things while bathing and dressing. She spoke frankly to herself while putting on her make-up, smiling and nodding while she anticipated her daily contacts. She gave absent people a piece of her mind when she was making the bed. She whispered who-knows-what while she was packing to go home from my house. An inveterate newspaper reader, she began to read articles quietly, lips moving rather quickly, then allowed the sibilants to reach the air, steaming out gently behind the curtain of the printed page. Her own voice reminded her what to think. We might say, it spoke to her.

An audience of one—that's what it boils down to at last—and why not? The spoken voice as the tender, the assistant, the repository, ready to call up the specifics, tell the brain what to think, believe, use for the present task.

Frankly I'm game for the spoken-aloud reminder. Right now I'm listening: "A dollar twenty-seven," "two cups of flour," "1207 West Main," "Jane Marie Spaghum," "July 27th at 10 a.m.," "blue, gold, and magenta."

Old Woman's Song from Mesa Verde
(migration tomorrow)

I lie down before the great lip
I have not gone out
from this lip of god
for twenty snows
Tomorrow I will not go

I cannot bear the thorns
the sunfire
the heavy way of walking

Tonight my jars are in place
The young ones in my keep
dream their tomorrow

Soon I am a rat
getting into my own store
out of season

Soon I wrap myself
in death skins

I sing my own death
with a small mouth.

Predictions

There will be droppings,
not the bird kind but
objects dropped out of hand.

There will be pickings up,
not like a vacuum cleaner,
but like a camel kneeling down.

There will be words
written without intestines,
some scrambled like breakfast.

There will be ideas,
precious and saved
for another rainy day.

There will be thoughts
intrusive, nagging,
best temporarily suspended.

Pre-need

So much work to death:
Will it be a cardboard box or reinforced steel?
Poplar, pecan, or oak...

although these latter cannot be sealed
since they are quite alive, still trees?
Thus, the issue is gasketed or ungasketed?

Gasketed is sealed, of course,
(like a jar of Grandmother's figs), and
"does not easily admit gravesite elements."

Heavens, no!—I don't want pink for the liner.
It must be ecru, or parchment or linen—
a color of paper, my favorite life surface.

Crepe is okay, or satin.
Last choice would be velvet—
because I'm prone to hot flashes.

As for the inner lid, No thank you
on the populars: Going Home,
Virgin of Guadalupe, or Christ of the Andes,

likewise the camouflaged liner
with the deer angel on the lid, special ordered
by a hunter who switched to cremation.

Now on to the final resting place—
Will it be "Gethsemane" or "Angel Field,"
"Mount of Olives" or "Garden of Peace"?

Take into consideration, in our area
there could be "drainage issues."
Thus, an inurnment? a mausoleum drawer?

And if it's ground burial, will it be side by side,
or stacked, and if so, how to decide,
like on warmer nights, who's on top?

Finally, the monument: marble, granite?
And of course if you will have been a Mason
or DAR, these symbols can be added.

No doubt, the way our sons grew up
questioning everything,
there will be some scoffing,

an abhorrence of the rituals,
especially the sentimental.
Still, take away the trappings,

including line items: guest book,
thank you notes, escort limo,
flower car, and these words:

"at the time of need,"
"whenever the service takes place,"
"issues," and particularly "situations,"

and how else are we to get died?

Suddenly...

        ...everyone is dying, going to Someplace.
I don't understand. Newly, I don't understand.
We're giving death reports to our children
the way we complained of our parents doing.
Age is knocking us up, a definite
tell-tale shade on the litmus,
formerly a speck not worth a squint.

Death's moved into the neighborhood,
made itself a welcome plate of brownies,
subscribed to the paper, built a pen for its dogs.
Lately, it's been going up and down the street
delivering letters on ways we can organize.
We're all addressed as "Resident."

Later

The child, now indifferent
to present company,
never dreaming he will be
anyone other than his present self,
is shown a petrified rock,
asked to listen to its origin,
feel it, marvel at its longevity.
He doesn't know that later,
on a hike, he will find
a mottled river stone, hand-size,
tumbled smooth by hundreds
of miles and several ages.
He doesn't know that he may,
later, much later, pick up
an old relative's journal,
finger the words in curiosity,
try to decipher where he came from,
each word a stoney clump,
each word entreating him
to find the right grip,
remember how his grandfather
taught him to hold the stone just so,
practice the swing, a little more now,
then skim it across the lake of his life.

Prognostication

There will be a light fog at first that will clear by mid-day
with only a scattering of high clouds. After noon,
you will notice you have written "participation" rather than
"precipitation." A 3-D landscape will feature the dowager's
hump, the stoop of the used-up back, and trailing feet.
Snow showers will prevail on the color of hair.
Lightning may flash on the retina, in which case the oculist
will prescribe drops since visibility will be limited.
Expect a large contingency of speckled trout
to arrive on the backs of hands. An approaching storm
in late afternoon will feature gusty winds into evening.
Falling rain will precede the falling of your friends all around,
and you. Two things to note: beautiful sunsets, except sundown
will be earlier than you would have wanted it.

Seasoned Love

What if two,
after long years of living,
after the depths and heights
of the heart's journey,
after the joy of having children,
after travels, situations,
friendships, failures,
triumphs and dreams—
what if two should
by happy chance
find each other?

Then, let them note
that sunsets show
the grandest colors,
that the open blossom
gives off the sweetest scent,
that only the tall tree
gives shade.

Let them delight
that rain is followed
by sparkling dew,
that thunder and lightning
bring the freshest air,
that a pale moon
may visit a dawning sky.

And let them content themselves
with laughter and stories,
with weaving their skills together,
with noting the seen and unseen.

Let them know
that they have received
a blessing full-fold,
and are to take the testimony
of love in all its strength
and bear it forward.

About the Author

Jan Seale is the 2012 Texas Poet Laureate. In addition to the twenty-eight books in various genres she has authored, her writing has been published in such venues as *Texas Monthly*, *Writer's Digest*, *Newsday*, *The San Francisco Chronicle*, and *The Yale Review*. Two of Seale's stories have been presented on National Public Radio.

She has held a National Endowment for the Arts Fellowship and has been a Humanities Scholar for Humanities Texas, as well as an Artist-in-the-Schools for the Texas Commission on the Arts. She holds membership in the Texas Institute of Letters.

A native Texan, Seale lives with her husband, John Brown, in the Rio Grande Valley of Texas near the international border. She has three sons and four grandsons.

www.ingramcontent.com/pod-product-compliance
Lightning Source LLC
LaVergne TN
LVHW090916290825
819731LV00020B/162